Living and Loving Life through THE LORD'S PRAYER

Terry Reed

© Terry Reed. All Rights Reserved.

Published by Relevant Pages Press. Charleston, South Carolina.

www.relevantpagespress.com
relevantpagespress@gmail.com

No part of this book may be used or reproduced by any means, graphic, electronic, or mechanical, including photography, recording, taping or by any information storage retrieval system without the written permission of the publisher except in the case of brief quotations embodied in critical articles and reviews.

Scripture quotations are taken from the following biblical translations:

Scripture quotations marked (TLB) are taken from The Living Bible copyright © 1971. Used by permission of Tyndale House Publishers, Inc., Carol Stream, Illinois 60188. All rights reserved.

Scripture quotations are taken from the Holy Bible, New Living Translation, copyright ©1996, 2004, 2007, 2013, 2015 by Tyndale House Foundation. Used by permission of Tyndale House Publishers, Inc., Carol Stream, Illinois 60188. All rights reserved.

Scripture quotations from THE MESSAGE. Copyright © by Eugene H. Peterson 1993, 1994, 1995, 1996, 2000, 2001, 2002. Used by permission of NavPress. All rights reserved. Represented by Tyndale House Publishers, Inc.

Scripture taken from the New King James Version®. Copyright © 1982 by Thomas Nelson. Used by permission. All rights reserved.
Cover design and interior layout by Bethany Smith.

ISBN: 978-0-9982211-2-0

Printed in the United States of America.

Contents

Forward by Joanne Ellison

The Launch

The Lord's Prayer... Matthew 6:9-13

Our Father..5	
Who Art in Heaven..14	
Hallowed Be Thy Name..19	
Thy Kingdom Come...24	
Thy Will Be Done...32	
On Earth as It Is in Heaven...40	
Give Us This Day Our Daily Bread.............................44	
Forgive Us Our Debts..51	
As We Forgive Our Debtors..55	
And Lead Us Not into Temptation..............................63	
Deliver Us from Evil..72	
For Thine Is the Kingdom, and the Power, And the Glory, Forever, Amen. *80*	
My Disclaimer...84	
The Names of God...85	

To Grayson, Noah, Lucy and Thomas,

Because I want you to know the love of "Our Father." Because I want you to understand the goodness of your creator. Because I want you to know from whence you come long before the world impresses upon you differently. Stand firm in your faith always. Run to God!

*Affectionately,
Your Oma*

FORWARD BY JOANNE ELLISON

God spoke to Terry in an unusual way or maybe not so unusual. Perhaps Terry was simply more open to hearing God in unexpected ways. She has set her heart on being prepared to hear from God daily and that is just what happened. For years she describes seeing the numbers on the clock at the exact time of 1:11 and 11:11. Determined to see if God was speaking to her, she found her answer in the Scripture Luke 11:1:

> *"Now Jesus was praying in a certain place, and when He finished, one of His disciples said to Him, 'Lord, teach us to pray as John taught his disciples."*

For years God had been prompting Terry to write a book on the Lord's Prayer, and now it was impossible to ignore the call. God was persistent and finally Terry heard and obeyed. His radical love and persistence and Terry's expectancy resulted in the book you are about to read.

Terry beautifully walks us through Jesus' prayer demonstrating the intimacy that Jesus desires for us; the same intimacy that He and His Abba Father have. He wants this close relationship with God the Father for us. As you walk through the pages of this book, you will encounter...

- A God who is holy (to be hallowed)
- A kingdom within
- Insights into God's will

- Bringing heaven to earth by our actions
- God's provision
- A path to forgiveness
- A cry for help
- A plea for protection
- And... a reminder that God's kingdom and power and glory are forever.

Terry's vulnerability and authenticity will draw you into desiring a closer walk with God. This book enables us to learn to pray the Lord's Prayer with sincerity and openness of heart. And.... My hope is that we will take Terry's example and look for God to speak in our daily lives—even the possibility of Him doing something so radical as speaking to us through the numbers on a clock.

THE LAUNCH

SURE ENOUGH, God spoke to me through a clock! I would never have listened had I still been a child. Time was unimportant to me then, but as an adult I'm constantly looking for and at a clock. I tell you this to make the point that we are preoccupied when it comes to time; some a little more than others. But most of us rely on our clocks. We live by our calendars. We have places to go, people to see, and things to do and it all happens around a clock. If it sounds like I am complaining but let me assure you I really am not. I'm actually grateful for clocks because they do help me maintain a (somewhat) organized life. Without one, I imagine in my mind that my world would be completely chaotic.

You are probably thinking right now, *"Why is she rambling on about time and clocks in a book about The Lord's Prayer?"* That is a very good question. Over several years, the frequent appearance of two particular times continuously got my attention. For about a year and a half to two years, I found myself glancing at the clock consistently at 1:11 and 11:11. This happened so much I began to mention it to my friends and quizzically ask them what it could mean. No one had an answer but I felt it happened way too much not to mean anything. So after pondering this for *years,* I finally decided to speak to God about it. "Duh," as my 4-year-old granddaughter would say! God pointed me to His Word, and pretty quickly, I might add.

Right after I'd heard from the Lord, my husband, Fred and I were flying to California for a short vacation. I had decided that on this five-and-a-half-hour flight I would begin to seek out what God was trying to tell me. Bible in hand, I boarded the plane prepared and willing to do some business with God. This was not my first rodeo with Him. He has walked with me and played with me before in sweet relationship, revealing both big and little things along the way. He cheers me on as I attempt to hear from him and understand His will. He gets me because He made me and He relishes in the excitement and joy I get out of His teachings and His playfulness. When my revelation occurred, the lesson revealed I was overwhelmed, overjoyed, and ecstatic and He knows I will tell anyone who will listen. Through our little moments, His name and goodness get spread to others. He is brilliant! He is contagious!

Seat belt fastened, tray-table down, husband beside me, and pen in hand, I opened my Bible to Genesis 1:11. There are 66 books in the Bible, many of them containing chapters and verses with the combinations of 1:11, 11:1, and 11:11, but I was determined to sift through each one and listen for the Lord. I'd set my goal and prayed God was in agreement. I had five and a half hours to figure this all out.

As I read through these chapters and verses in Genesis, Exodus, Leviticus, Numbers and Deuteronomy, I was no closer to understanding what God was trying to tell me. None of them resonated in my spirit when I read them. And I was sure God would alert me if I ran across something I was to set aside and contemplate. A little discouraged, I closed my Bible and said a quiet prayer. "This is getting me nowhere, Lord. Can you help me out please?" I felt a prompting to go directly to the New Testament books and skip the rest of the Old Testament, so I did just that. I started with Matthew and Mark but nothing stood out. But then I came to Luke. Luke 11:1 reads:

> *"Now Jesus was praying in a certain place, and when He finished, one of His disciples said to Him, 'Lord, teach us to pray as John taught his disciples.'"*

Then, further into Luke, I found Luke 11:11:

> *"What father among you, if his children ask for a fish, will instead of a fish give him a serpent."*

I took note of those verses and continued on my path through the New Testament. Finally, in the last book of the Bible, Revelations, God could not have been clearer. Revelations 1:11 reads:

> *"Write what you see in a book...."*

That's when it all came together for me. For several years, I had felt God prompting me to write a book on The Lord's Prayer. I'm not a writer by profession, so I wasn't sure what to do with that prompting. To be quite honest, I just ignored it for years. After this, I couldn't ignore it any longer unless I wanted to live in complete and utter disobedience to God. Since I didn't want to separate myself from Him by living outside of His will for me, right there, on that airplane, I made a commitment to God to prepare, study, and write the book He wanted me to write. *This* book. God and I had hashed it out in the heavens on an airplane in five and a half hours! I hope this book brings you as much joy and peace in the reading and studying of it as it gave me writing it!

God Bless!

Terry

CHAPTER 1

Our Father

IN THE BIBLE, God is referred to by many names. Jesus refers to Him in The Lord's Prayer as "Father", or more accurately, "Our Father." Whose Father is He? He is my Father and your Father.

We are all created by God but to become a child of the Living God we must "confess with our mouth that Jesus is Lord and believe in our heart that God raised him from the dead, and we will be saved." (Roman's 10:10.) This is when our adoption as children of God takes place. We become a part of God's family through *"faith in Jesus Christ."* (Galatians 3:16.)

But are we all really His children? Throughout scripture God refers to us as His children: 1 John 3:1 reads:

"See how much our heavenly Father loves us, for He allows us to be called His children and we really are."

John 1:12 reads:

"But to all who believed Him and accepted him, he gave the right to become children of God."

Ephesians 1:5

"God decided in advance to adopt us into his own family by bringing us to himself through Jesus Christ. This is what He wanted to do and it gave him great pleasure."

What is our Heavenly Father like? One of the things I find comforting is that Our Father never changes. He remains the same through our bad times and our good times. We can count on Him to be consistent and reliable. I am sure we all have a testimony about the imperfections of our earthly father, and God understands our earthly fathers are fallible, that they make mistakes and He still loves them. But we need to understand that God, our Heavenly Father, is perfect and infallible. He never changes. He is:

Omniscient -

He knows everything. Psalm 147:5

"How great is our Lord? His power is absolute! His understanding is beyond comprehension!"

Omnipotent -

He has no limits. Nothing is too hard for Him. Matthew 19:26

> "But Jesus looked at them and said, "With man this is impossible, but with God all things are possible."

Omnipresent -

He is always with us. Psalm 139:7

> "I can never escape from your spirit. I can never get away from your presence."

Unchanging -

Malachi 3:6

> "I am the Lord, and I do not change."

Forgiving and Merciful -

Daniel 9:9

> "The Lord our God is merciful and forgiving even though we have rebelled against Him."

Loving -

John 3:16

> "For God so loved the world that He gave His one and only son, so that everyone who believed in Him, will not perish but have eternal life."

Truthful -

Titus 1:2

> "This truth gives them confidence that they have eternal life, which God, - who does not lie - promised them before the world began."

Faithful -

Psalm 89:8

> "O Lord God Almighty, who is like you? You are mighty, O Lord, and your faithfulness surrounds you."

Our list of the nature, characteristics, and goodness of our Heavenly Father could go on forever. No one has been creative enough or imaginative enough to come up with the one descriptive, all-encompassing word that would describe in completeness who Our Father is. So, we will continue to use the many words we know and the new ones we will learn about Him through our own life experiences. I will add a few other descriptions from my own list of ways He has helped me. He has molded my thoughts and my heart for him by being my provider in times of need, my strength in times of weakness, my comforter in times of grief, my counselor when I had nowhere to turn, and my peace when my spirit was lacking. I trust Him for all things.

Our Father is good all the time. He loves us all the time. He is not angry or hateful. He is not thinking of a way to punish us when we mess up. He is looking for us to trust Him and turn to Him in all things.

We are to lay our burdens at His feet. I prayerfully hope after reading this first chapter you will go confidently to Him in all things trusting that "all things work together for the good of those who love God." God, I'm thankful I'm your child and you are my Father.

A Note from Terry...

Before I was touched by the world and all of its influences, I knew there was a God. As an innocent young girl, I knew God loved me and I loved Him. This connection for me was somehow natural.

As I got older, the world began to creep in and I fell prey to the influences of other people, the media and worldly views. I had moments of closeness with God but many moments where I drifted away from Him and His love. Some moments were very long. Like for *years.*

It wasn't until seven years ago that I came to understand the true character of God and how much He loved me. He wasn't a God waiting on me to sin so He could punish me. He loved me and wanted a relationship with me.

As I studied Him through His Word, my love for Him began to grow again. He had never stopped loving me or pursuing me. I had walked away from Him. I had stopped pursuing Him. I continued to call myself His but lived a life of voluntary disobedience. I ignored what little bit I knew about Him, his laws and commandments because much of the world said it was ok to. I was a people pleaser, not a God pleaser.

I lost decades of time and suffered much pain because of the way I lived my life away from God. This way of life failed me over and over again. I looked to fill the void I felt with things, titles, and people. I was a nice person, living a life controlled by my fleshly desires, not by The Holy Spirit. I listened to my peers who said it was okay to drink alcohol until you passed out. It was okay to have sex before you marry. It was okay to lie to your parents. None of this is okay. That belief system is of the world and not of God.

I was one of the lucky ones. I had parents who paid attention and took me to church and did all the right things. My father was an amazing, kind man who would have done anything in the world for me and my brother. He truly was a top notch dad and a man of great integrity. There was a time when he had a stroke and was in the hospital for 5 weeks. One of his biggest concerns when he got home was to honor God with the tithing he had missed when he wasn't able to attend church. He scribbled out the amount he paid each week and multiplied it by the number of weeks he had missed and took it to church the following week. He was faithful and trusted God's Word. He had a quiet spirit and a quick dry sense of humor. He never yelled. He took me fishing. We had picnics and lazy summer days in the country. He was gentle and nonjudgmental. I was fully (well *almost*) known and accepted by him. It was easy to be with him.

Through a time of several losses in my life, one of them being the loss of my father, I began to seek God. In this time of excruciating pain, I knew and understood if I was going to survive this time with anything in tact it would have to be through something bigger than a counselor, pastor or a friend. I would turn to these people for support but I instinctively knew God was the only source of what I needed - a whole life transformation.

In this deep time of sorrow when everything in my life was going wrong, I began to read His Word and study Him. I knew He sent His only son to die on the cross to save us but I never considered that it meant me too. Me personally, me independently. Somehow in my mind I had separated myself from the grouping.

My mindset of exclusion is one of the lies Satan wants to use to keep us trapped. He does not want me or you to believe we could ever be the object of God's affection. He wants us to believe we could never be good enough to be loved by God. He knows if we start believing in God's love for us individually and who we are to God because of Jesus's sacrifice on the cross, he's got trouble. We might just start to realize the abundance and depth of all He has for us and our calling to increase His Kingdom. That is a calling on all of our lives and one I won't ignore any longer. Bigger and better than any job I can think of.

So one day at a time, one seed at a time I will continue to plant the reality of His great love. I consider Him in everything I do, all of my thoughts, actions and words. I am by no means perfect. I fall short every day. The difference now is that I recognize those failings. If I don't catch myself first before I slip and align myself with God then I repent and turn back to Him, seeking a renewed relationship.

He is always on my mind and he lives in my heart. He is not just a passing thought or a theory. He is my Father-my Heavenly Father. The same Father I looked up to as a little girl and accepted with no proof.

I was blessed with a wonderful earthly father. Maybe your luck of the draw, at no fault of your own, was a father who drank too much and ignored you. Or maybe you had a father who physically abused your mother and maybe even you. Maybe your dad walked away and left you abandoned and devalued. Maybe you were sexually abused. Or maybe your father chose to not be involved in your life at all. These are all painful experiences and no child ever deserves to be treated that way. None of that was your fault. My heart overflows with compassion for you. It breaks my heart and it breaks God's heart. What we long for is to be loved and accepted by our parents, not pushed away.

Gratefully, there is one thing we can count on: We have a Heavenly Father who's even better than the very best earthly father. A Father who loves us so much He sent His only son Jesus to die for us so we could have a relationship with Him. Our Father in Heaven is bigger than any problem, any insecurity, any hurt, any sadness, any sickness. When you get to know Him and you cry out to Him, He will come to you. He speaks and guides us through His Word, His Holy Spirit, and His people.

No matter your experience, your Father God loves you. Cry out to Him. He will be your strength, your comfort, your peace, your miracle, your all-sufficient one. He knows your needs and he will meet you where you are. Psalm 18:6

> *"In my distress I called to the Lord; I cried to my God for help. From His temple he heard my voice; my cry came before Him, into His ears."* KJV

CHAPTER 2

Who Art in Heaven

LIGHT AND BILLOWY. Crisp air. Warmth from the sun on my back. Flowers everywhere. Latticed pergolas. Thick green grass. Puffy white clouds. Rolling Hills. Lots of sheep. White robes on everyone. Cool streams running over smooth stones. Very quiet. Peaceful. That was my vision of what Heaven was like before I looked in the Bible.

What does Heaven look like according to the Bible? For starters, the Bible tells us there isn't just one Heaven, but three. In Genesis 1:1 it speaks of God creating the "Heavens" (plural). In Deuteronomy 28:12 God calls His "Heavens" His good treasury. The three Heavens are divided like this: The First Heaven is the earth's atmosphere. This encompasses the sky, the air, the trees, the birds, and the clouds. It's where we live and breathe. Spiritual beings exist here as well. Angels and demons dwell in The First Heaven. The angels are on missions from God and demons are trying to trip us up using the tactics of The Father of Lies.

The Second Heaven is what we would call outer space. It consists of the sun, the moon, stars and planets. The Third Heaven is the place where God dwells and where His Throne Room is located. The First and Second Heavens are visible to the human eye, but we have to go to the Bible to get a description of The Third Heaven.

The Third Heaven, God's dwelling place, is the city where His Throne Room is located. Revelations 21 and 22 speak of the beauty of this place. There is a wall of every kind of precious stone including jasper, sapphire, agate, and emerald. There are gates of pearl, streets of gold, clear as glass. God's glory lights the city. There are no more nights. A river of living water sparkling like crystal flows from the throne of God down the middle of the gold street in the city. The tree of life is on both sides of the river bearing 12 kinds of fruit. That is certainly a tree I can't wait to see. Can you imagine you are out for a little country walk and you happen upon a tree that has pears, apples, lemons, grapes, oranges, grapefruit, peaches, plums, raspberries, blueberries, figs, and blackberries growing on it? Truly amazing!

As happy as I will be to see the wonderful things in Heaven I will also be happy to shed some earthly things. Revelations 21:4 says,

> *"He will wipe away every tear from their eyes, Death will no longer exist; grief, crying, and pain will exist no longer, because the previous things have passed away."*

No struggles, no sadness, no fear, no Satan, no hunger, no deceit, no lies, no temptation, no separation, no divorce, no abuse. All bad things cease to exist. Our Father is good!! There will be fellowship, peace, joy, contentment, laughter, love, honesty, goodwill, and (I'm really hoping) animals. All good things.

Is there anything you long to be free of on the earth? I sometimes long to be free of my schedule. I overschedule myself and end up with very little free time just to be. I'm going to be perfectly fine letting go of my calendar. Hallelujah, Amen.

God promises everlasting life to His children who have come to Him through His son Jesus Christ. He dwells in Heaven but He is everywhere all of the time. He is in us so Heaven is in us as well. Right here, right now, while we are still on this earth, Heaven is in us.

A Note from Terry...

I prayed for God to reveal to me a moment in time or a personal story about Heaven. I haven't been there, so I don't have one.

The very next day, as I turned the corner, there was a work truck parked on the street near my house. On the back windshield in big white letters, "Only One Way to Heaven" was sprawled across every square inch available.

I have lived in this neighborhood for eight years and in this town for the same amount of time. I've never seen this truck before. I wondered if I had stopped and asked the owner when he put "Only One Way to Heaven" on the back of the truck would he have probably told me it was the day before? A couple of verses instantly came to mind:

There is only one way to the Father in heaven and that is through Jesus Christ, His son. John 14:6,

> "Jesus said to him, "I am the way, the truth, and the life. No one comes to the Father except through me."

Acts 4:12,

> "and there is salvation in no one else, for there is no other name under heaven given among men by which we must be saved."

And that is Jesus. This is not me talking but Almighty God spelling it out for us in His instruction manual. I believe His words, all of His words, to be without error.

This truck was no coincidence. This was God talking to me about what He wants me to share on Heaven, where He dwells, what is on His heart. Eternal life in Heaven comes through Jesus Christ only. By grace we are saved, not by works. I find it humorous that the message "Only One Way to Heaven" was on the back of a work truck. Once we come to know and love the Father good works come from the overflow of love God bestows on us. You cannot earn your way into heaven by good works though. There is no amount of work on this Earth, or rule-following, that will get us into heaven. But I can tell you that is my life goal. Under heaven, not part of my plan.

In Heaven, I want to visit with God and Jesus and all my loved ones who have gone before me. That is promised to me. If I love God with all my heart and all my soul and all my mind and next I love my neighbor, then God says heaven is in my future.

CHAPTER 3

Hallowed be Thy Name

As a kid I never understood the word "hallowed." What does it mean? To my child's eyes, it looked an awful lot like "hollow" but "hollow" means to be empty. I knew God wasn't empty. Even as a child I knew He is full.

Now, as an adult, I have studied and researched this part of The Lord's Prayer at length. I'm no longer looking at this through the eyes of a child, but as an adult seasoned by the events of life. Experience gives us a new perspective on the significance of His holy name. Thy name, His name is understood to be holy, glorified, sanctified, and revered. It is to be honored and respected, adored and lifted up high above all else, because He is to be high and lifted up. His name represents His character and His character is who He is. Essentially, His name is as

Holy as He is. Read that again: His name is AS HOLY as He is. He is the "Great I Am," "The King of Kings," "The King above all Kings." He is "The Almighty." He is "Magnified,"! His name is above all names and is worthy of praise.

Growing up in the sixties and seventies I rarely heard anyone curse or swear using The Lord's name. I memorized the Ten Commandments in Sunday School and knew the third commandment said,

> *"You must not misuse the name of The Lord your God. The Lord will not let you go unpunished if you misused His name."*

God's name is not to be dirtied or defiled. However, today in our society, it is common for people to use the Lord's name in vain. I take this very seriously and believe Him when He says I will not go unpunished if I misuse His name. That produces a healthy dose of the fear of the Lord in me.

I believe that the fear of the Lord is a good fear. It just means for us believers that we extend to him reverence and awe. We believe what He says. We understand that He despises sin and He is a just God. We understand just as our parents need to discipline us from time to time that God has that same relationship with us. He is Our Father and we are His children. Discipline is part of that relationship. A healthy fear of the Lord and receiving of His correction has diminished in modern society.

Likewise, the practice of consciously honoring the name of the Lord has decreased in modern society as well. How do we worship and honor God in our daily lives today? As a family, do we pray together? As parents, are we teaching our children about the love of God and the importance of Him in our loves? As kids, do we leave God out of our decisions and our activities with other kids? Are we speaking of His character, His strength, His power, and His love regularly, or are we not speaking of Him at all? Are we teaching the next generation what it means to truly revere God's holy name? Ephesians 5: 1 and 2 offers us a way to bring glory and honor to God's name:

> *"Imitate God, therefore in everything that you do, because you are His dear children. Live a life filled with love, following the example of Christ. He loved us, and offered himself as a sacrifice for us, a pleasing aroma to God."*

Maybe it's time to focus on honoring the name of the Lord in our daily lives and teaching the next generation what that means. A healthy fear of the Lord will keep us and our children safe and protected under His wings.

A Note from Terry...

Holy is His Name. Holy, Holy, Holy!

Funny Story: In my travels I was fortunate enough to spend six days with complete strangers from Australia. We met up in France and happened to be sharing the same tour guides. I could not have picked anyone nicer, funnier, or sweeter to spend time with than these perfect travel partners. At one of our dinners together, I had the privilege of sitting next to one of these ladies and getting to know her better. In her lovely Australian accent, she asked me what I did. I told her I had many people in my life - such as my kids and grandkids - who I spent a lot of time with. I also told her Fred and I have the great honor of being able to minister to couples who are struggling in their marriages about the hope Jesus offers. She stopped me right there and said, "Why Terry, you do know you are speaking to an atheist, don't you?" I understood that what I did and said at this time would be very important. I have witnessed many Christians turn their backs on non-believers as if they were less than and not worth their time. They would rather hang with those of like-mind. That is not necessarily bad, but we (as Christians) should look forward to the opportunity to share Jesus and the gospel.

I heard someone at a conference once say we are always "blessing the blessed" and "serving the served." Let's start looking for opportunities to spread the love of God to those who do not know him. It's our job. So at dinner, in this very awkward moment, I decided to brush her unbelief off as a side note and build a relationship with this lovely lady. Keep in mind, she also had a choice to make here. She could have decided to brush *me* off and find someone else to sit next to at our dinners, vineyard tours and hikes. Much to my surprise, she didn't.

One day during our travels we went to Casis, a scenic seaside town on the Mediterranean Ocean. As we got off the bus and stood staring at this beautiful clear turquoise sea, my new friend said, "Oh my God." My husband directly said, "Exactly."

During the rest of our trip she and I spent many hours strolling through vineyards speaking of our families and our pets. It was so lovely and so natural. I pray that I represented Christ well and gave her enough that it softens her unbelief and leads her down a new path. I would like to think I "hallowed" His name through my actions. That somehow, I brought honor and glory to His Name and my new friend saw Jesus through me.

CHAPTER 4

Thy Kingdom Come

Revelation 21:2 Reads:

"And I saw the new city, New Jerusalem, coming down out of Heaven from God."

IN THE END, His Kingdom will come, and it will invade Earth. And there will be a new Earth. While we wait for this new Earth, a different kind of invasion is taking place for those who love Him. When I invited Him to live inside of me something big happened. I didn't consider what it would mean for my heart, mind, and soul; I just knew I'd be changed forever. The invasion of God's Kingdom inside of me rocked my world. I became His Kingdom on Earth.

We gain all things good when we turn over our lives to Christ and live with His Kingdom in us. It's the everlasting joy through all situations and circumstances. It's the peace that passes all understanding. It's the freedom to let go of past hurts. It's the strength to forgive others as we just couldn't before. A different life lays before us as we journey to becoming all He intended us to be.

Changes begin to occur in our lives once He comes to live inside of us. We love and serve and give like never before. Our selfishness begins to melt away. We start to see things as God sees them, and our heart breaks for what breaks His. We live out joy and peace. We trust totally in the sovereignty of God, His supreme authority. We give up our own wants and desires and put God in the driver's seat.

I am His and He is mine. I have His ear; He hears my prayers. I talk to Him and He listens. He loves me without condition. He knows the desires of my heart. He is with me all of the time. I become an adopted daughter, a citizen of Heaven, and so do you.

We are new territory for the Kingdom of God. The world we live in wants to encroach upon the ground we have gained. Circumstances and situations in life will want to intrude and break the boundaries that have been established in God's name.

Free will has been given to us by God. We've chosen Him. Now we have new choices to make in this life. As a new creation in Christ, how are we going to handle tough situations and times when peers are pressuring us to do what we know in our hearts is wrong? We all have a desire to fit in and be accepted. But sometimes the right thing is not always the easy thing.

1 John 3:7 says,

> "Little Children, let no one deceive you! The one who does what is right is righteous just as He is righteous."

Galatians 6:7-10 says,

> "Don't be deceived! God is not mocked. For whatever a man sows, he will also reap, because the one who sows to his flesh will reap corruption from the flesh, but the one who sows to the Spirit will reap eternal life from the Spirit. So we must not get tired of doing good, for we will reap at the proper time if we don't give up."

The choices we make once we have chosen God are just the beginning of sowing and reaping in our lives. The relationship between sowing and reaping is very important. I have witnessed devastation in others' lives and my own when I've ignored these words. We are always sowing seed into something, and eventually, we will reap what we've sown. We can't be careless. What we allow to be sown into our lives is extremely important and it makes an impact in ways we can't ever imagine. When we sow well we are protecting the Spirit within us.

When we don't sow well and live out our sinful nature or fleshly desires the Holy Spirit mourns and gets quiet. He doesn't work in us when we are living unholy lives. What we allow into our minds and bodies should not defile the Holy Spirit that lives inside of us.

We all have tough decisions to make in this life. Let your walk be worthy. Be the light in the darkness. Shine so all the world can see that the Kingdom of God has taken up residency in you.

A Note from Terry...

Yes, our Father's kingdom is coming and we should get ready. We don't know the date and time of the second coming of Jesus Christ. We don't have the luxury of that knowledge. My husband and I minister to people in a marriage enrichment ministry and sometimes we ask the question, how sure are you that you would go to heaven if the world ended tonight? When we ask we get different responses. Some are absolutely sure, some have the deer in the headlight look and some honestly say, I don't know. We have to get right with God. We want to be on that narrow road.

While we are waiting for "Thy Kingdom Come," we have many opportunities to live out His kingdom right here on this earth. I want to share with you a few selfless acts people I know have done to serve others. This is His kingdom in operation here on Earth. God's kingdom here involves transformed hearts. Transformed to operate out of love, compassion, understanding and the knowledge of hope that comes only from Jesus Christ.

- *There was a young man with a gift card to spend and he heard a prompting from the Lord to give his gift card to a lady he saw walking up and down the aisles at Wal-Mart. He did it without question and she began to cry. She used the money to purchase a gift for her granddaughter for Christmas! He happens to witness the purchase, and see the joy in the grandmother's face as she tells the story to the check-out* girl. He leaves Wal-Mart with an overflowing full heart like he had never experienced. He was truly the one who was blessed.

- *My dad loved to fish and spent many weekends fishing in my great aunt's ponds. After a long day of fishing, he would clean the fish, bag them and take to a family of eight who lived in a house with dirt floors. They had no stove and cooked outside over a fire. My dad got them a stove at some point.*

- *My grandchildren once witnessed their granddad walk outside of the McDonald's and give money to a homeless man to come in and eat. He took him by the arm and walked in with him and helped him order. The impact it made on my grandkids will last a lifetime.*

- *A young boy I know raked leaves for an elderly woman in the neighborhood. Her hope was restored.*

- *There are many people who participate in the act of paying for the order of the person in the drive-thru line behind them. I've been the recipient of this and it made me want to act generously and pay it forward.*

- *I've seen caring people whose kids are grown sacrifice their own Saturday night after a hard week of work to watch the children of a young couple so that couple could go on a much-needed date.*

- *I know many, many people who sponsor a child through Compassion, touching the world in Jesus's name.*

- *Some grandparents are paying the tuition for their grandkids to attend a private Christian school. These grandparents want to give their grandkids a foundational beginning to their life, for them to know Jesus and know they are loved by God. Don't feel discouraged if finances don't permit this in your family, not everyone can do this. Teaching children about God can be done everywhere.*

- *I know a group of women who donate their time to cook meals for a single moms group and their children every week. The moms bring their kids to study the word of God and everyone shares a meal. This is one night that these moms don't have to stress over preparing a meal for their family or even being able to afford to feed their family; the one night they can let go and be served.*

- *Even the act of selflessly spending hours at a time with someone telling them of your brokenness and how God has restored and healed you provides hope.*

God uses ordinary people for His good works on this Earth. He used David to kill a giant with one little stone and a sling shot. He was a shepherd boy who was looked down upon even by his family, he did the unbelievable. And when we do the unbelievable, God gets the glory.

If you want to do extraordinary things for God, it starts with prayer. Pray something like this:

> *Dear Heavenly Father, help me open my eyes to see the hurt in this world and help me to recognize those times when I can provide hope for someone else. I ask for a heart desiring what God desires and eyes to see His Kingdom in operation here on this Earth. In Jesus' name, Amen.*

What can you do today to show God's Kingdom here on Earth? Look for the opportunities! Do the unbelievable for the glory of God!

CHAPTER 5

Thy Will Be Done

IT'S EASY TO SAY "Thy will be done." But, how do we know what the will of God, Our Father, truly is? The simple answer is we have to get to know Him to truly know His will. We have to understand his nature and his character. We need to develop an idea of Him based on His words and His actions.

We sort of do the same thing when we chose our friends. We (hopefully) examine or study a potential friend. We look at their behavior and actions. We notice if she lifts others up or tears them down and then we make an educated decision on whether we will accept them as a friend or steer clear. We know that a friendship can impact our lives in big ways so we take great care to learn about the people we've selected to be our friends.

We need to study God not to accept or reject Him, but to know Him. If we want to know God and His will for our lives intimately, we have to learn about Him through His Word. We have to read the Bible. Second

Timothy 3:16 says,

> "All Scripture is God-breathed and is useful for teaching, rebuking, correcting and training in righteousness."

His laws and rules are for our benefit so we may live to our fullest potential on this earth. As a young girl, the 10 Commandments were my first look at what God wanted for me. It was an easy place to start to begin to know His will for my life.

The 10 Commandments

I AM THE LORD YOUR GOD. YOU SHALL WORSHIP THE LORD YOUR GOD AND HIM ONLY SHALL YOU SERVE.

YOU SHALL NOT TAKE THE NAME OF THE LORD YOUR GOD IN VAIN.

REMEMBER THE SABBATH AND KEEP IT HOLY.

HONOR YOUR FATHER AND YOUR MOTHER.

YOU SHALL NOT KILL.

YOU SHALL NOT COMMIT ADULTERY.

YOU SHALL NOT STEAL.

YOU SHALL NOT BEAR FALSE WITNESS.

YOU SHALL NOT COVET YOUR NEIGHBORS WIFE.

YOU SHALL NOT COVET YOUR NEIGHBORS GOODS.

In the New Testament, Matthew 22: 36-40, God says,

> *"You shall love the Lord Your God with all your heart and with all your soul and with all your mind. This is the great and first commandment. And the second is like it: "You shall love your neighbor as yourself."*

He goes on to say that if we live out these two commandments, then all of His laws are covered. With these commandments, we have a good start at understanding His will. Other places to study God's will is in Proverbs and Ephesians. They are full of God's instruction on His will for our lives. Several examples are as follows:
Proverbs 28:7 says:

> *"Young people who obey the law are wise: those with wild friends bring shame to their parents."*

Proverbs 29:11 says,

> *"Fools vent their anger, but the wise quietly hold it back."*

Ephesians 4:26 says,

> *"And don't sin by letting anger control you. Don't let the sun go down while you are still angry for anger gives a foothold to the devil."*

I would like to clarify here, God is for you and not against you. His instruction and commands are designed to protect us and teach us. Living in obedience to His laws and instructions allows us to have a full, honorable, and peaceful and joy filled life. God only wants the best for His children.

Satan, however, hates you. John 10:10 tells us that Satan comes to kill, steal and destroy us. And he won't give up, he is persistent, yet powerless stacked up against God. Nothing good comes from Satan.

The problem for all of mankind is our will does not always align with GOD'S Will. To submit ourselves to Christ we have to give up our will. We have to live in obedience and be willing to turn over all control to Him. This is His Spirit living inside of me directing and guiding me in everything I think, everything I do and in everything I say. No more self-centeredness. No more selfish ambition. No more me, only God. I am His, all of me. I must die to my own desires so that His Spirit can take the reins and lead me in his ways.

Our lives work better when we are submitted to His Will instead of our own. He can do immeasurably more than we could ever hope or imagine in our lives. And He desperately wants to. Our desires for ourselves would look small in comparison if we could see them next to God's desires for us. His will for us is big and we are insignificant without Him. Our purpose is directly connected to Him and has been created by Him. Apart from Him, we have no purpose. We need only listen to know His will.

Jesus is a great example of someone following the will of the Father. John 6:38 says,

> *"For I have come down from heaven not to do my will but to do the will of Him who sent me." When Jesus went into the garden of Gethsemane to pray before He was about to be captured by the Roman Soldiers He asked His Father: "Father, if you are willing, take this cup from me; yet not my will, but yours be done."*

Jesus knew what He was facing yet He wanted to do only the will of His Father.

Following the will of God isn't always easy. Sometimes it's painful and is counter to everything we would do left to our own devices. I heard Billy Graham once tell the story how God spoke to him about His will for Billy Graham's life. Young Billy Graham had been courting a girl he loved very much and assumed would be his wife. One day, God told him she was not the one. Billy was heartbroken when He heard God tell him he had to break it off with her. Through tears Billy did what he believed was the unimaginable, he broke up with the girl he loved because it was God's will. Years later he met his wife Ruth and realized God had been right. God had a different plan. God has blessed Billy Graham and his family their entire lives because Billy Graham is a man who chases after the heart and will of God.

We always have a choice. It is called "free will." We can decide to follow Christ and do His will or we can rebel against it. One looks great, the other one not so much. Are we going to be a God pleaser or a people pleaser? I am convinced that the reason a lot of people avoid a personal relationship with God is because they know there is work and a journey involved. They may have to change some things in their life. It's too much work. But what we need to remember is that just like in Billy's life, we gain so much more than we could ever lose when we follow the will of God. And what we lose, we end up being grateful for losing anyway.

God's will calls us to action for His Kingdom. I believe the world will be changed through the believers that chose His will over their own. So, as we stand in church and say the words, "Thy will be done," we need to give thought to what they may mean. His words have life and shouldn't be ignored. His will is perfect. His love for me makes me long to be obedient. If He truly has taken up residence in my heart then His Holy Spirit in me presses me to want, more than anything, the will of My Father.

A Note from Terry...

I heard a story once about a man who broke the law and was thrown into jail. He would serve his time and get out, only to break the law again and go back to jail. Most of his life was spent repeating this cycle, until one day he decided to try something different. He decided to study the law so he could avoid jail. He spent years and years studying the law. Thousands and thousands of laws he committed to memory but it didn't matter. There was no way he could ever know every law ever written in this world. He would land back in jail every time.

Then someone shared with him the gospel and he fell in love with Jesus. He read in the Bible of God's two greatest laws. Matthew 22:37-40 reads,

> *"You must love the Lord your God with all your heart, all your soul, and all your mind. This is the first and GREATEST commandment. A second is equally important: Love your neighbor as yourself. The entire law and all the demands of the prophets are based on these two commandments."*

The man realized at that moment he could have saved a whole lot of time, energy, and effort. All he needed to know were these two laws. Not the thousands he had committed to memory and ended up back in jail anyway. He committed to focus on these two laws from Matthew spoken by Jesus and he served no more jail time ever. Loving God and loving your neighbor cleans things up a little bit. Psalm 119: 97-99 when I think on God's laws:

"Oh how I love your law. I meditate on it all day long. Your commands make me wiser than my enemies, for they are ever with me. I have more insight than all of my teachers, for I meditate on your statutes."

As this man learned, spending time meditating on God's laws rather than man's is time well spent.

CHAPTER 6

On Earth as It Is in Heaven

How can this Earth we live on look anything like Heaven? Heaven is good and Earth is broken. In Heaven there is no sin, no disease, no torment, no pain, no sadness, no anger, and no death. On Earth, there is all of these and much, much more.

There is hope in these seven words, *"on earth as it is in Heaven."* If Jesus said it, then it must be possible. Jesus never made impossible requests of us. If He said we could live out heaven here on Earth, then it must be so.

First, let's examine why our world is messed up. It all started with Adam and Eve and the temptation of the serpent. When God created The Garden of Eden, He filled it with anything and everything Adam and Eve would ever need. He told them they could eat from any tree except The Tree of Knowledge of Good and Evil. The serpent tricked Eve, and she and Adam ate from the tree. When they did this, sin entered into the world and the Earth became Satan's domain. That sin, "original sin," is why our world is so broken. The earth will remain the domain of Satan until the second coming of the Messiah, Jesus Christ.

On Earth, there is a war going on for our souls. The Bible warns us that on this Earth, we will have trouble. Satan will try to trick us with his lies and deceit. He is very clever, so we have to be alert. He prowls around looking for someone to devour. He comes to us in our thoughts and uses little whispers such as, "it's ok to do it, everyone else does", or "You deserve it, you work hard.", or "Go ahead, you can cheat just this once."All are lies and all are part of his scheme to destroy you. Satan is very active in alcohol and drug abuse and pornography. He understands addictions are hard to break and can destroy generations after us, but our God is big. He can help us beat anything.

God always provides us with an escape from our sin. We don't have to fall into the traps of Satan. 1 Corinthians 10:13 says,

> *"No temptation has over taken you that is not common to man. God is faithful, and He will not let you be tempted beyond your ability but with the temptation He will also provide the way of escape, that you will be able to endure it."*

God will not, however, force you to do the right thing. He will never compromise your free will. He lets us make the choice. God loves us and wants us to love Him in return. He is God; He could force us to love Him. But God understands in order to have a real relationship with us, our love for Him has to be a choice. When we make the choice to love God, our minds are transformed and renewed. Paul says in Romans 12:2,

> *"Do not be conformed to this world but be transformed by the renewal of your mind that by testing you may discern what is the will of God, what is good and acceptable and perfect."*

Heaven on Earth is us doing our part to make the world better. We become Heaven. We heal others of disease and sickness and we cast out demons, all in the authority of Jesus by the power of the Holy Spirit. We become the light in dark places, we destroy evil in the world. We share the good news of our Lord and Savior with others while on this Earth. We walk differently, we talk differently, we even look different. Psalm 34:5 says,

> *"Those who look to Him are radiant, and their faces shall never be ashamed."*

When we are truly walking in the Spirit we affect everything and everyone around us. We are heaven on Earth. We live joyfully and triumphantly, without fear. We live as conquerors because of what Jesus did on the cross at Calvary for us.

A Note from Terry...

The only way heaven can exist on this Earth at this time is through God's people. Isaiah 65:17 reads:

> *"See, I will create new heavens and a new earth. The former things will not be remembered, nor will they come to mind."*

Do you want to "create" change in the world? Do you want to make it so "the former things aren't remembered" and help create a new reality for those here on Earth? Then put God in the center of your life and focus on one person at a time. Do it by the way you live by the word of your testimony, and by the way you love those around you. If you have a story that would bring hope to someone who is hopeless, share it. That is heaven on Earth.

One day we will experience a new heaven and a new Earth. True freedom from all bad things will come. In the meantime, God will use ordinary people like you and like me to do extraordinary things on this Earth for His Kingdom. And to God be all the Glory!

CHAPTER 7

Give Us This Day Our Daily Bread

I LOVE BREAD! I eat it daily, sometimes several times a day. God knows the importance of feeding ourselves. He provided Adam and Eve with the food they would need. When the Israelites were in the desert and had nothing to eat He provided manna and water. Nehemiah 9:15 says,

> "You provided bread from heaven for them for their hunger. You brought forth water from a rock for them for their thirst."

And let's not forget the miracle of the five loaves and two fishes. Jesus fed 5000 plus using the five loaves and two fishes gathered from the crowd following Him. He knows the importance of food to feed and nourish the physical body.

After forty days and nights of fasting in the wilderness, Jesus was hungry. Satan tempted Him using food. Satan said, "If you are the Son of God, tell these stones to become bread." Jesus knew it was more important to follow the word of God than to feed His body. Jesus answered,

> "It is written: 'Man shall not live on bread alone, but on every word that comes from the mouth of God."

Basically, food is important but God is who truly sustains us.

In the world we live in today, we work so we can have food to sustain our physical bodies. The money we earn provides food. But we also use our earnings to buy things that will make us temporarily happy. Most of us understand our physical needs, but how many of us even consider how to feed our spirits? Are we addressing that at all?

I neglected my spiritual needs for many years. I believe many of us do. What part of our lives are we giving to God? Is it zero minutes a day? Ten quick minutes a day? One hour a day? Ten hours a day? All 24? I've learned over the years the importance of seeking the Lord with all my might and all my strength all day long. My day goes so much smoother when I start with feeding my spirit the "daily bread of His word" and then the "daily bread of prayer." I then focus on the "daily bread of making the conscious choice to think good thoughts instead of bad thoughts." He gives us everything we need to connect with Him spiritually. We can connect with Him from sun up to sun up, 24/7, but it requires seeking and focus.

Matthew 7: 7-8 says,

> *"Ask and it will be given to you; seek and you will find; knock and the door will be opened to you. For everyone who asks receives; the one who seeks finds; and to the one who knocks, the door will be open."*

Matthew 6:33 says,

> *"Seek ye first the kingdom of God and His righteousness and all these things shall be added unto you."* *If we seek God first spiritually in all things, we can trust that our daily bread or all of our needs will be met. God will provide.*

Each week at my church, we have what we call a "response time" after the message. Our pastor asks us at the end of the message, "What is God saying to you, and what are you going to do about it?" There are several ways we can "respond" to God during that time. We have a cross people can pin a petition or prayer on; we have candles that can be lit in prayer or for remembrance, and we have prayer intercessors who stand along the back wall ready to pray for anyone who has a need. Some people even come back to pray a prayer of thanksgiving because they have experienced a breakthrough. The fourth response is the one I really want to draw attention to though. It's the act of Holy Communion.

Each week as I put the bread in my mouth I think of how Jesus's body was broken for me, and how He took on my sin so I could have a relationship with The Father and the promise of eternal life. This is strong, and a sacrifice beyond anything I could ever imagine. During The Last Supper, in Luke 22: 7-38, Jesus said this as He broke the bread,

> *"This is my body which is given up for you. Do this in remembrance of me."*

Now as we come to Him in remembrance of what He did for us on the cross we can be assured that whoever believes in Him, their spiritual hunger will always be satisfied. God gave us Jesus; He is God's bread for us. Jesus is my bread every day in all things. John 6: 35 says,

> *"I am the bread of life. Whoever comes to me shall not hunger and whoever believes in me shall never thirst."*

Are we starving for the bread of God? Are we starving for His peace and joy and contentment? Or are we looking for the world to feed our spiritual needs? The world can never feed us; that is quite literally a dead end. The world can never fill the hole in our hearts. We try to fill that hole with things such as another person, a new car, alcohol, drugs, lust, and the list goes on. What we are really missing is the daily bread God gave us in His son Jesus. We just need Jesus!

Wherever I go and whatever I do, my desire is to represent Jesus, His character and His nature. It's the change that makes us live differently. I cannot say I love Jesus but then behave selfishly and without compassion and love. If I love Jesus, good works will flow out of that transfer of love. His love for me and my love for Him presses me to serve others. I want to do good things for other people. I want to leave Jesus in my wake.

When I decided to love God in this way and follow Jesus, things changed in my life. I find it hard to be around people who are self-serving, self-indulgent, and without compassion. Negativity is a big downer for a true follower of Christ. Just like I can't feed myself unhealthy food and expect to remain healthy, I can't feed my spirit ungodly food and expect to remain godly. We need to spend time with people who are equally yoked and of like mind. We need to remove the bad influences in our lives and find new, good influences. Pray that God will place those equally yoked, like-minded people in our lives and that we continue to feed ourselves with God's daily bread.

A Note from Terry...

Bread. I *love* bread. I love to eat bread. But there is no bread as satisfying as God's Daily Bread. When I ignore my hunger to get into His Word and focus on Him, I begin to notice it. I don't handle situations as well, my kindness slips, my personal edge gets sharp, choices become harder to make because my spiritual vision is fuzzy, and lines between right and wrong are often blurred.

Without God's Daily Bread, I become spiritually lacking and ravenous for Him and His Word. I don't need His Bread just once a week or three times a week, but every day. Then, and only then, can I endure the trials I will face. His bread gives me peace, love, joy, patience, and kindness and all of the fruit of the spirit. I run to Jesus to get my portion of His Bread and I feast on it. He is my source of life.

When my spiritual blood sugar runs low and I'm hungry for His word, I take the time to read my Bible and pray a prayer like this:

Dear Heavenly Father,

Thank you for Your Word. I run to it in times of joy, times of heartache and times of great need. You are the answer to all things. Just as you supplied the Israelites with manna from the heavens while they were in the wilderness, you provide me with sustenance through Your Word. I thank you that you love us so. In Jesus Name, Amen.

Take the time to feast on God's Daily Bread before you feed your physical body man's bread, and you will be a healthier whole person than you could ever imagine.

CHAPTER 8

Forgive Us Our Debts

I WAS HURT very badly by someone once, and out of that hurt came a strong fleshly desire to hurt back. I felt I was justified. It was done to me, so I wanted them to experience hurt too. I hear sentiments like this in conversations when someone will say, "I guess I told him." while puffing themselves up in pride. I've witnessed people say and do awful things in a spirit of revenge and retaliation, while never thinking twice about it. The attitude of the world is if they hurt you, then hurt them back harder.

People end up in big messes and sometimes jail because of this kind of attitude. There are people who have lived their entire lives this way without considering once that they may be in sin. The debt these people are building up is a debt that will be owed to God. That is scary to me. Fellowship with God is impossible if we are living this way. 1 John 1:6 says,

> *"So we are lying if we say we have fellowship with God but go on living in spiritual darkness; we are not practicing the truth."*

We are not speaking of debts in terms of financial debts here, although we can certainly sin where our finances are concerned. The debts we are talking about in The Lord's Prayer are our sins against God. Our sins of "commission" meaning our deliberate sins, and our sins of "omission" meaning the failure to do something we know we should do. Both are considered debts owed to God.

We are all sinners and we sin in all kinds of ways. Often, we sin secretly so as not to be judged by others. However, the judgement we should be most concerned with should be the judgement of our almighty Father, who seeks justice in all things. God sees and knows everything we do in private and in front of others. Sometimes we sin because of peer pressure; we want to be accepted and a part of the crowd. Sometimes we just can't help ourselves and we do something that is wrong and don't care that we have done it. The problem lies in a lack of a good, healthy dose of the fear of the Lord. The Bible tells us we will all stand before The Judgement Seat of God one day. So our daily lives and the way we live them do matter. Our daily decisions, big and small, are important.

The good news is God loves us and longs to be in fellowship with us. He had His Son Jesus, who walked the earth without sin, die on our behalf. How this must have broken His heart. Jesus took our sin on the cross in a horrible death all so our debts could be cancelled. Our past, present and future sin/debt was cancelled with Jesus's blood, sweat and tears. He paid our ransom! Thank you, Jesus.

We serve a God who is faithful, merciful, and grace-filled. He wants to forgive us! If we confess our sins to Him, He will be faithful and cleanse us from all wickedness (1 John 1:9).

If Satan had his way, God wouldn't have come up with a plan to save all of His children. Satan would have preferred us be in complete rebellion against God. John 10:10 says,

> "The thief comes to kill, steal and destroy."

Satan's complete plan is for us to live our eternal lives in Hell. He continuously schemes against us, looking for ways to lead us into failure through temptation. God is much smarter than Satan though. You see, upon Jesus' ascension into Heaven He left us a gift. He left us the gift of the Holy Spirit and we now have authority to resist Satan and his tactics to kill, steal and destroy us. James 4:7 says,

> "Submit yourselves, then, to God, Resist the devil and he will flee from you."

Satan is merciless and his power over us was extinguished at the cross. He will continue to tempt us and strategize against us but we are no longer controlled by him (Romans 6: 6-7).

This forgiveness of our debt that we receive from God and recite in The Lord's Prayer comes directly from God's mercy. We are totally dependent on "Our Father" in Heaven for this forgiveness we seek.

Without His forgiveness and His grace, we would be instead faced with God's wrath of anger, punishment, judgement and Hell. We would deserve it too. God, our good, good Father, sent His only Son in sacrifice where He took on all of our sin. He actually became our sin. His body was broken and His blood spilled so our Father in Heaven could have a forgiving, loving relationship with us, His children.

Our sin can be compared to the physical dirt and mud we are covered in from hard labor outside. Our family owns a tree farm and after a good rain we will often go out and get some work done. We do extensive physical labor in big mud puddles and then come home covered head to toe in mud from our day. Tired, worn, heavy and weary we carefully find our way to the shower. We strip off the heavy water and mud soaked clothes and boots and step into a very warm shower.

As the mud, dirt and grime rinses off and finds its way to the drain I am reminded that as a sinner I am weighed down by my sin. I am heavy, tired and worn from this rebellion against my God. I bare myself in repentance to Him and He washes me clean. All my spiritual mud (the things that hold me back and separates me from Him, specifically my sin) has been washed down the drain. I am as clean as the white driven snow. That nice warm shower sure feels good but nothing compared to the renewing of my soul. God Is Good! I hope we tell Him how grateful we are every day for His forgiveness of our debts.

However, for all of our debts to be forgiven, we must remember God requires something from us.

CHAPTER 9

As We Forgive Our Debtors

THE TWO SCRIPTURES below show that forgiving others is a requirement if we want to be forgiven. This is pretty serious stuff. It is a command from God, not a mere suggestion. Matthew 6: 14-15 says,

> *"For if you forgive men when they sin against you, your heavenly Father will also forgive you. But if you do not forgive men of their sins, your Father will not forgive your sins."*

Luke 6:37 says,

> *"Do not Judge, and you will not be judged. Do not Condemn and you will not be condemned. Forgive, and you will be forgiven."*

When someone hurts us or hurts someone we care about, what is our typical response? Is it one of quick forgiveness? When we recite The Lord's

Prayer and we ask God to forgive us by saying, "Forgive us our debts," we are thrilled He is willing to do that for us. But there is a second part to that petition. It's a part scanned over quite quickly by most of us because it's not always easy. We must also forgive others.

Forgiveness of others debts (wrongs) against us isn't as popular as our own forgiveness. It's hard to forgive sometimes, especially immediately following the hurt. Some people hold on to the offense for years and some, even for life. God says forgive quickly so as not to give the devil a foothold (Ephesians 4:27). Mathew 5: 23-24 says,

> *"Therefore, if you are offering your gift at the alter and there remember that your brother or sister has something against you, leave your gift there in front of the alter. First go and be reconciled to them; then come and offer your gift."*

True forgiveness is letting go of all offense. We are to get rid of bitterness, anger, rage, harsh words, and slander, as well as all types of evil behavior. (Ephesians 4: 31). When we choose not to forgive as God commands, the anger and bitterness hardens our hearts. It is difficult for someone with a hardened heart to give love or receive it. It causes trouble in one's life and pollutes many people.
Hebrews 12: 15 says,

> *"See to it that no one falls short of the grace of God and that no bitter root grows up to cause trouble and defile many."*

How many times must I forgive the same person? Let's look at Matthew 18: 21- 22. It's a conversation between Peter and Jesus:

> *"Then Peter came to Him and said, 'Lord, how many times could my brother sin against me and I forgive him? As many as seven times?'"*
>
> *"'I tell you, not as many as seven,' Jesus said to him, 'but 70 times 7.'"*

Jesus was saying that forgiveness is unlimited when true repentance is the case.

Forgiveness requires humility and gratitude. Forgiveness says: you owe me nothing and I will not dwell or hold on to the wrong you committed against me. Even if the person never apologizes to you, it is saying: I will not hold any resentment whatsoever. It is saying: Even though I am feeling heartbroken, resentful, angry, bitter, and a whole host of other things, I will, instead, take on the nature of God and act with grace and mercy, just the same as God shows me.

In our humanness, we reject the idea of forgiveness. We want to hold on to the anger, rage, and resentment. Our human nature sometimes even goes as far as acting in retaliation. Our human nature is very closely related to Satan at times. He loves it when we lose control and act out in sin. His goal is to separate us from God, not to mention to kill, steal and destroy us. Repaying evil for evil is wrong.

In Romans 12: 17 God says,

"Do not repay anyone evil for evil".

We are to give it up to God.

Forgiveness is not excusing what someone did or condoning the action. Forgiveness is not a feeling and it doesn't feel natural. It goes against everything that makes sense in this world to us. It doesn't mean that the hurt and pain you feel isn't real and justified. It doesn't mean you are weak and have no backbone. Instead it is the most courageous thing you may ever do. When you do it, you will do it with the supernatural strength of the Lord behind you. "I forgive you" may be the three most difficult words you will ever say, but they may also be the three most important words you will ever say. What comes after saying these three words is an overwhelming sense of freedom.

Right behind the freedom comes the peace and joy that is unexplainable but what we all long for. Don't wait for the memory of the offense to be dulled before you forgive. God says do it quickly. Ephesians 4: 6 says,

"Do not let the sun go down on your anger".

Remember forgiveness is not forgetting or saying that what the person did is ok. Forgiveness is an agreement with "Our Father". He understands the importance of the condition of our heart. There is nothing in the Bible that He tells us to do that is not good for us. He wants our hearts soft and pliable so we can be free to give love and receive love. A bitter heart can do neither.

Forgiveness doesn't mean the other person goes unpunished either. Rest assured that God will deliver justice in His way and in His time. He says in Romans 12: 19,

> *"Friends, do not avenge yourselves; instead leave room for His wrath. For it is written, vengeance belongs to me, I will repay says the Lord".*

He is just as angry and hurt that you, His child, were wronged.

After we forgive, the next step is to try to reconcile with the other person. Sometimes reconciliation isn't possible if the other person hasn't taken responsibility for the hurt. There was a time in my life where I forgave a wrong against me, but reconciliation wasn't possible. The other parties didn't accept responsibility. But, I definitely forgave them.

The final step is a tough one but it's a sure sign Christ lives in your heart: pray for your enemies. God tells us in Matthew 5: 44 to love and pray for those that persecute us so that we may be sons of our father in Heaven. Someone once put this in perspective for me when they reminded me that while Jesus died on the cross to forgive me of my sins, He also died on the cross to forgive the sins of those who have hurt me. If God has forgiven them of the sins they have committed against me why am I still holding onto them? It does me no good, in fact it keeps me in bondage.

On your spiritual journey if you find you are stuck, examine your heart and see if there is any forgiveness being withheld from someone. Make it a practice each day to forgive anyone that has offended you during that day and move forward in the freedom that is gained when you turn it over to God.

A Note from Terry...

Have you ever held on to a hurt? Have you rehearsed what you would like to say to get back at the person who hurt you? I am guilty of both of these things. Forgiveness will poison and consume you. Your thoughts will lean towards impurity. Negativity becomes your central dwelling place. This is a bad place to be.

Forgiveness offers us peace and freedom. It's an agreement made between you and God. Matthew 6: 14-15 reads,

> *"For if you forgive other people when they sin against you, your heavenly Father will also forgive you. But if you do not forgive others their sins, your Father will not forgive your sins."*

Matthew 5: 44 tells us to love your enemies and pray for those who persecute you. We are to be seekers of love in all things.

I once held on to unforgiveness for an entire year. It consumed me. My thoughts were about retaliation. It was on my mind every minute of my days. I couldn't escape it. My heels were dug in and I was not going to let their offense go. It had hurt too bad and had threatened my family. I felt forgiveness was letting them off the hook. But it wasn't at all. It was letting me off the hook.

When I finally got smart enough to do what God was telling me to do all along, things changed. My forgiving them brought joy back to me. I doubt very seriously if they cared that I hadn't forgiven them anyway. Then as time passed I began to pray for them. I prayed for their hearts to change and for them to become lovers of Christ. I don't know if that has happened but I do know that I was obedient. I may run into them one day and if I do, I can only pray that I will shine the light of Jesus regardless of the journey they may be on. Reconciliation is not always possible but forgiveness is.

CHAPTER 10

And Lead Us Not into Temptation

THIS LINE is more of a cry for help from God's people. Jesus understands our weakness and our sinful nature, so perhaps this is His way of reminding us to ask Him for help every day. The original Greek word for "temptation" used here means "trial" or "testing." So when Satan is tempting me, it is a trial or test. He is enticing me toward evil. My plea is that God gives me the strength to separate myself from Satan's tests and to follow Jesus's example.

When God allows Satan to tempt me in any area of my life I have two choices. I can succumb to the temptation or sin and find myself separated from God or I can choose not to give Satan any ground. I can instead discern the danger of failing the test and turn to God to give me the strength to walk away from the sin. When I choose to turn my back on the sin and be obedient to God's word I am blessed.

What Satan intended for evil and to use against me, God then turns into good in my life.

When I turn from sin and act in obedience to His Word, He is pleased and I am refined. He refines me through each test. Then when I respond in obedience and faithfulness, He uses me for His kingdom on Earth. I find it to be such a privilege that the Lord of the Universe would use me for anything. I am so grateful.

I know we have spoken in previous chapters about Satan's plan to kill, steal and destroy us but it deserves repeating. It needs to be understood that he is working every day against us. He lives to devour us. The stronger your walk is with God the harder Satan's pursuit of you. You are your own worst enemy. 1 Peter 5: 8 says,

> *"Be sober-minded: be watchful. Your adversary, the devil prowls around like a roaring lion, seeking someone to devour."*

He never takes a day off. Some common names for him are prince of darkness, the deceiver, the evil one, the accuser, the adversary, anti-Christ, beast, devil, enemy, father of lies, Lucifer, wicked one. None of these conjure up anything I want to be associated with.

He entices us to sin in three areas:

1. *Lust of the flesh - taste, touch, smell, and hearing*

2. *Lust of the eyes - seeing*

3. *Pride of life - self-elevation*

When we are living in the flesh these are the areas where Satan will grab us. Our bondage starts in the mind and is born out of selfishness and fleshly desires. Romans 8: 6-8 says,

> "The mind governed by the flesh is death, but the mind governed by the Spirit is life and peace. The mind governed by the flesh is hostile to God; it does not submit to God's law, nor can it do so. Those who are in the realm of the flesh cannot please God."

We are in constant battle between the flesh and the spirit. Our flesh results in death. Living in the Spirit in accordance to God's word, out of love, brings life and peace.

Now that we understand the areas in which Satan will tempt us, it is most important to understand that God never allows Satan to tempt us with anything we can't bear and that God will always provide a way of escape, according to 1 Corinthians 10:13. And when we remain faithful, "Our Father" will reward us. Stay strong in your tests and trials and stay firm in His Word and you will be blessed.

Alone, without God, we cannot stand against Satan and his tactics. He will win every time. God gives us a visual of what we need to do each day to protect ourselves. He uses the metaphor of a Roman soldier's armor. Ephesians 6:12 tells us who the battle is against.

> "For our battle is not against flesh and blood, but against the rulers, against the authorities, against the world powers of this darkness, against the spiritual forces of evil in the heavens."

Ephesians 6:13 says,

> "This is why you must take up the full armor of God, so that you may be able to resist in the evil day."

The armor of God gives the believer all he needs to hold his ground against the evil one.

The Armor of God

The Belt of Truth - the truth of God's word

The breastplate of righteousness - righteousness of God along with living a good life

Feet shod with preparation of the gospel of peace - a readiness to spread the good news

Shield of Faith - the confidence in the Lord - when the flaming arrows of the evil one comes at us, they are deflected with the shield in the belief and confidence in the Lord.

Helmet of Salvation - the believer knowing that the victory is his (our salvation)

The Sword of the Spirit - this is God's word - not meaning the whole Bible, but scripture that meets the circumstance

Remember every event, every trial, every test in our life is molding us. Remain steadfast, resist Satan's temptations, continue building your character to resemble the character of Christ Jesus who lived as man and never sinned.

Remember God gave us the gift of repentance. Because we are not perfect, when we fall, we must reunite ourselves immediately with God through that gift of repentance. Turn from the sin and face the Lord. Do not let sin defeat you and separate you from your God, who wants to lavish His love on you. There is no shame and condemnation in those who love Christ Jesus. His blood on the cross covers those who love Him. He took all of our past, present and future sin. We no longer have to live by the law but we live instead by the freedom of God's redeeming grace. Romans 6: 14 says,

"For sin shall no longer be your master, because you are not under the law, but under grace."

A Note from Terry

When I am tempted, I think of it as a test. If I pass the test which usually involves obedience to Christ's word, then I like to believe I might get promoted and get to move on to the next thing God needs me to deal with. There is so much in me that needs to be fixed or sharpened but I know He is faithful and He loves me. First Corinthians 10:13 reads,

> *"No test or temptation that comes your way is beyond the course of what others have had to face. All you need to remember is that God will never let you down: He will never let you be pushed past your limit: He will always be there to help you come through it."*

I trust that He will help me work through all the brokenness. I trust that He will help me in my temptations and tests. All I need do is ask for wisdom and strength. I won't pass the test every time, but I will try to run the race well.

However, sometimes I am weak. I give in to a lie from the evil one. He whispers in my ear that what I'm about to do is 'OK.' Or, he tells me, that I'm only satisfying a curiosity. Or, that no one will know. Or, (and this is a good one) he tells me, that I deserve it. Whatever it is, it's always a clever lie. Sometimes I forget that my identity is found in Christ and I actually fall for the lie.

It's much like a time when I was four years old and I was on the Bozo the Clown Show on TV. All the kids were sitting in rows in bleacher seating. Cameras were rolling and Bozo walked up to me and asked me my name. With his microphone stuck in my face, I froze. Seconds, which felt like minutes, went by and he asked me if I had forgotten who I was. Quickly, to take the spotlight off of me, I said my name is Terry Beamguard Teresa Carroll. When put to the test at the age of 4 I had forgotten who I was. My real name was Teresa Carroll Beamguard (before marriage). My nickname was and is still Terry. I can tell you, Bozo was as confused that day as I was. He said to me, that's an awful lot of names and he moved on. I was so embarrassed. I remember the feeling of wanting to shrink and not be seen. Stage fright had taken over and at the age of 4, for a brief moment, I had forgotten who I was.

Many, many, times over the years, I've forgotten who I am. I don't mean my name, but spiritually, I've forgotten who I am. I love God so much but sometimes my weaknesses burst through. I have many weaknesses but recently my most prominent weakness showed up and I fell for it. Satan attacked my identity.

Through a simple conversation I'd had with someone important in my life, the enemy of my soul led me to a place of pain and division. It's a place I thought I'd long left behind. But I took the bait, and feelings of anger, confusion, jealousy, heartbreak, mistrust, and insecurity rushed over me. I was told (by Satan once again) that I'm absolutely and utterly powerless over the events in my life. I was told that I'm not enough. Not pretty enough. Not young enough. Not smart enough. Not interesting enough. Not anything enough. I spiraled down into a very familiar pit that years before had almost swallowed me. I look back on it now and I can't believe I fell for it again!

I thank God every day for the gift of the Holy Spirit. You and I both received him upon Jesus' ascension into Heaven. In the middle of my downward spiral that I spoke about, a bright light on my personal dashboard was flashing red: Alert! Alert! A great dose of conviction, correction, counseling and warning washed over me. I heard in my spirit, a voice so sweet and so kind say, "Terry, have you forgotten who you are?" My answer was: "Yes, Holy Spirit, for a brief moment, I did."

When we are tempted, we need to remember whose we are and who we are. We belong to God. He is our creator. As believers, our identity isn't based upon what we do but on what was done for us by Jesus on the cross. Because of His suffering, we have been adopted into God's Kingdom as sons and daughters. (Ephesians 1:5). Scripture says in John 1:12 we are children of God brought to fullness in Christ. (Colossians 2:10). We are Christ's friend. (John 15:15). We are set apart and appointed as prophets. (Jeremiah 1:5). Our bodies are temples of the Holy Spirit. (1 Corinthians 6:19). We are holy and blameless. (Ephesians 1:4). We are no longer a slave to sin (Romans 6:6). We have been set free. (Galatians 5:1). We are Chosen. (1 Peter 2:9).

When temptation comes your way, remember who you are in Christ. Remember that you are loved and, in your times of weakness, remember who to turn to. Remember your sin has been washed clean and Jesus is always interceding on your behalf. As a believer, you are no longer in the grip of the evil one but are held firm by God. (1 John 5:18-21).

When we fall to temptation, we need to remember God is always there to receive us back. We just need to recognize our sin, repent, and align our hearts with His. He has enough grace for us all. I want to end with Ephesians 2: 4-5. It reads,

> *"But God is so rich in mercy, and He loved us so much, that even though we were dead because of our sins, He gave us life when He raised Christ from the dead. It is only by God's grace that you have been saved."*

Ephesians 2:8 reads,

> *"God saved you by His grace when you believed. And you can't take credit for this; it is a gift from God."*

Dear Heavenly Father,

Help me to choose the path that you would have me walk Lord. Help me to steer clear of Satan and his plans to throw me off course. Help me to recognize his lies. Give me wisdom, Lord, for I know without you I am powerless. I love you Lord and I pray that in my walk I don't lead someone else to stumble into temptation. In Jesus Name, Amen.

CHAPTER 11

Deliver Us from Evil

WHO ARE WE FIGHTING AGAINST? Ephesians 6:12 tells us our battle is not against flesh and blood, but against the rulers, against the authorities, against world powers of darkness, against spiritual forces of evil in the heavens.

Our battle is not against each other but instead against something much more terrible. And it's something we can't even see. Just like God has a plan and purpose for our lives, Satan also has a plan for us. He comes to kill, steal and destroy. He means us evil and harm. He has not a compassionate bone in his body. He loves it when we hurt, when our marriages fail, and when we die before we give our lives to Christ. Satan is a liar and an accuser. He operates in our thought life He is the whisper that says you're not good enough, the thought that says God could never love someone like you. He mixes a little truth with a lot of lies.

Satan convinces you that you are not worthy of love. He is everywhere - in our homes, our workplace, our churches. He is the ruler of the world we live in and he wants us destroyed. He and his wicked counterparts or demons have tremendous power. He is a very slick trickster. He is the one who throws temptation our way. He sets the bottle in front of the person struggling with alcohol, he puts the needle in the heroin addict's arm, he makes sure sexual images are flooding and popping up in front of the person struggling with pornography. He puts the food in front of the person with an eating disorder and the stores all around the shopaholic. Satan has the *power* to destroy our lives but he does not, and I repeat, he does not have the *authority* unless we give it to him.

As Christians, demons cannot live in us but they can oppress us and mess with us. If we go up against Satan with only our own power and strength, he will win every time. But as true believers of Christ, the battle is already won. Jesus won that battle for each of us on the cross. His blood covered all of our sin and now we can live in complete freedom. We are no longer bound by the sin of the world but are set free by the love of God who sent His Only Son to die on the cross so we may live.

After Jesus died and was resurrected, and before His ascension into Heaven, he left us a gift from the Father. He left us the gift of the Holy Spirit. With the Holy Spirit we have the authority to come against the schemes and wiles of the devil. This is not all the Holy Spirit is or does once He takes up residency in us. We now have God's Spirit leading our Spirit. We are born again. Without being born again, we don't have salvation. We cannot have salvation without being born again. When the Holy Spirit is living in me I am born again and am assured of salvation. When the Holy Spirit comes to live in us we become the temple of God. We are set apart or different from the people of the world (the unbelievers).

The Holy Spirit is a person. In John 16:13 the Holy Spirit is described as a "He." He has a will. In 1 Corinthians 12:11 He delivers gifts as he determines. He has a mind. In Romans 8:27 using His knowledge of the Father he intercedes for us. He also has feelings. In Ephesians 4:30 the scriptures say that the Holy Spirit is capable of grieving. He is our counselor, our comforter, our helper, our advocate, and our intercessor. He is always available in an emergency. He equips us. In 1 Corinthians 12:1 it speaks of his gifts to us. He enlightens us. In John 14:26 Jesus tells the disciples not to worry about all the information He had just given them. The Holy Spirit would remind them. Romans 8:15-17 speaks of how he enriches us and in Ephesian 3:16 it speaks of him empowering us.

Galatians 5: 22-23 tell us about the fruits of the Spirit. He gives us joy and peace, patience, kindness, faithfulness, gentleness, love and self-control. He gives us boldness to witness. He gives us wisdom and revelation. He speaks to us and through us in prayer.

The Holy Spirit is a big deal. Do we tap into him and the power he has or do we rely on our own strength and answers? As I said earlier, we are toast against Satan without the power of the Holy Spirit. We need to give the full house over to the Holy Spirit. Do not keep any part of ourselves separate from him. He is our wind and he will direct us into the will of God.

To be delivered from evil, we must use this amazing gift from Christ. We have to stay connected. We can do this by practicing faith. He doesn't say we have to have a boatload of faith to please Him. There is nothing wrong with a boatload of faith but He can honor small faith as well. Faith the size of a mustard seed can move mountains. That is very encouraging because we all know our faith levels can fluctuate based on our situations and circumstances. We need to stay in God's Word to know the hope found in Jesus and the promises of our Father. If we aren't reading His word, it's like driving a car without a steering wheel. Nothing makes sense.

We can also be delivered from evil through prayer. We have to let prayer invade our life. The power that comes from this communication with The Father is beyond anything we could ever describe. We should enter into our prayers with thanksgiving and gratitude for all He has done in our lives and all He is going to do. Receive it with a gracious heart. Seek His answers and wisdom for everything in your life and ask Him for the desires of your heart.

Come into agreement with our Father in your prayers using His Word and your words. He is not concerned with the prettiness of our prayers or the bigness of our words. He is not concerned with the number of words we use. Sometimes I think He would just like us to get to the point and stop beating around the bush. Pray boldly, expecting to hear from God. He is interested in your heart, your needs, and your wants. He is interested in everything about you. Don't be afraid to share with Him the good, the bad and the ugly. He already knows it and He is waiting for you to knock, seek and ask.

By using the authority Jesus left us in the Holy Spirit against Satan we can surely cast him aside. I did not learn this until I was 51 years of age. I shudder to think of all I could have avoided in my life had I been instructed and taught about spiritual warfare. You can rest assured my children know, my grandchildren know and anyone else I run across who I can tell. People don't like to talk about Satan and he loves that. He is happiest when we don't believe he exists because he is able to keep wreaking havoc in your life undetected. When we know he is there, we can use the power of the Holy Spirit and the instruction of God and beat him every time. He is persistent but we will prevail because of the blood of Christ. It's as simple as this, but you must say it out loud. Satan can't read our minds. He spends most of his time filling our minds because he can't read them.

Here is what you are to command:

> *"In the authority left to me by Jesus Christ, I renounce you Satan and I come against any plan you have to hurt or destroy me. I resist you and command you to go! In the Holy name of Jesus Christ. Amen".*

A few scriptures you may want to memorize to use when you may feel vulnerable or under attack:

> James 4:7 Resist the devil and he will flee from you. [NLT]

> Isaiah 54:17 No weapon formed against you shall prosper, and every tongue which rises against you in judgement you shall condemn. This is the heritage of the servants of the Lord, and their righteousness is from me, says the Lord. [NLT]

> Luke 10:19 I have given you authority to trample on snakes and scorpions and to overcome all the power of the enemy; nothing will harm you. [NLT]

> 1 John 4:4 you are from God, little children, and have overcome them; because greater is He who is in you than he who is in the world. [NLT]

A Note from Terry...

Is there some kind of evil that has penetrated your life? We live in the world and evil is all around us. But we have a Deliverer and because of Him we don't have to live in the darkness of evil. Evil was beaten by Christ's victory on the cross.

Although Christ has defeated evil, it's up to us to claim that victory by rebuking evil when it tries to invade our lives. We have to command evil, out loud, to be gone in the name of Jesus Christ. Luke 10:19 reads:

> *"Behold I give you the authority to trample on serpents and scorpions, and over all the power of the enemy, and nothing shall by any means hurt you."*

Philippians 2:9-10

> *"Therefore God has highly exalted Him and given Him the name which is above every name, that at the time of Jesus every knee shall bow, of those in heaven, and of those on earth, and of those under the earth."*

I have experienced evil in my life and seen evil in the lives of others. Our God is bigger than all of it. We need to remember that establishing a life of resistance to evil will cause Satan to flee from us.

Just remember, be strong in the Lord and in His mighty power. Ephesians 6:11-18 says:

> *"Put on the full armor of God that you may be able to stand against the wiles of the devil. For we are not fighting against flesh and blood enemies, but against evil rulers and authorities of the unseen*

world, against mighty powers in this dark world, and against evil spirits in the heavenly places. Therefore, put on every piece of God's armor so you will be able to resist the enemy in the time of evil. Then after the battle you will still be standing firm. Stand your ground, putting on the belt of truth and the body armor of God's righteousness. For shoes, put on the peace that comes from the Good News so that you will be fully prepared. In addition to all of these, hold up the shield of faith to stop the fiery arrows of the devil. Put on Salvation as your helmet, and take the sword of the Spirit, which is the word of God. Pray in the Spirit at all times and on every occasion. Stay alert and be persistent in your prayers for all believers everywhere."

Victory is ours because of Christ's sacrifice on the cross. Let us never forget that.

CHAPTER 12

For Thine Is the Kingdom and The Power and The Glory Forever and Ever. Amen

THIS LAST SENTENCE of The Lord's Prayer was a later addition by the church. It was not part of the prayer Jesus taught the disciples in Matthew and Luke. The Catholic Church still does not use this as part of their prayer. This part of the prayer is called a "Doxology" which is a hymn or form of words containing an ascription of praise to God.

As I meditate on this last line from The Lord's Prayer, I find myself mourning over the death of King David. I have never had this kind of reaction to any other of the great men of the Bible before other than for Jesus himself. Why David? Why now?

To look at David, one can see he understood the goodness and the greatness of our God. He operated out of deep feelings of love, thankfulness and trust. David was not perfect. He committed horrible things and suffered consequences because of them. In the end though he had a repentant heart and sought out God. He chased Him for he loved Him so much. He danced before the Lord. He spent time alone with God. He wrote beautiful songs and praises. He was a man after God's own heart.

Why is it hard for us to reach that place in our relationship with God? I don't know exactly why but I'm going to venture out here and I'm probably going to be a lot wrong and maybe a little right. In our busy, busy lives, maybe we keep God on a surface level. In order to have a relationship with the kind of depth David's relationship had, we must become vulnerable. We live in a culture of self-reliance and control. We are afraid to let go for fear of being too known. If I'm too known, I might not be accepted and I want to be accepted. This may carry over from our personal relationships on Earth to our relationship with God.

In his last days, David speaks before the assembly of leaders about The Lord. In 1 Chronicles 29:11-13 David tells of his love for The Lord.

> *"Yours, O Lord, is the greatness and the power and the glory and the victory and the majesty, for all that is in the heavens and in the earth is yours. Yours is the kingdom, O Lord, and you are exalted as head above all. Both riches and honor come from you, and you rule overall. In your hand it is to make great and to give strength to all. And now we*

thank you, our God, and praise your Glorious name."

My grandkids will sometimes ask me: "How big is God?" I will answer them: "He is super big, so big that I can't describe it." But in the passage above, David does a decent job of it.

Do I believe He is all of these things? And if I do, does that shape my behavior? Have you heard the song by Mercy Me, *I Can Only Imagine*? I ponder what I will do as I stand before The King of Kings and The Lord of Lords, as I stand before God Almighty. I hope I will honor him and show my love for Him the way David modeled in his relationship with God. What about you?

God came into my heart through a painful situation and He is there to stay. I can't imagine my life without Him now. I know what it was like before, without direction, confused, jumping from thing to thing, and empty, seeking permanent joy in temporary things.

God sacrificed His Son so we could have a relationship with Him. He wants to lavish us with multiple blessings. He wants to talk with us and be present in our lives - in the little things as well as the big things. I will do what He desires for me to do. I will spend time with Him and I will commune with Him and pay attention to Him, seeking what direction He would have me go. I will praise Him in my struggles and I will trust He will turn them all to good. Why? Because He loves me.

I want to have His character. I want to be His hands and feet. I long to completely surrender to

Him, to give my life that I may live. Matthew 16:25 says,

> *"For whoever wants to save his life will lose it, but whoever loses his life because of Me will find it."*

So where did this last line of The Lord's Prayer originate? In 1 Chronicles 29:11-13, David ended his prayer with the words:

> *"...for thine is the kingdom, and the power, and the glory, forever and ever."*

I like that this is where the church found this verse to add to the end of The Lord's Prayer. I like that it came from King David – the man after God's own heart. It is a perfect ending to a perfect prayer. The words are a great reminder of who we are praying to and that He is not temporary but everlasting. Amen, so be it!

My Disclaimer...

Father God,

Forgive me if I have added to or taken away from anything in your Word. It was not my intention. I'm not a biblical scholar, I'm just a girl in love with you and seeking to be obedient. You know my heart. The last thing I would want to do is tarnish the words that you so beautifully transcribed to all the great writers of your Word.

Father God, I love you so much and I believe you wanted me to write this book. If it draws one person who is lost in this world, feeling hopeless, closer to you, then it was time well spent. May God get the glory!

Amen

Names of God

EL SHADDAI

(el shad-di')

All-Sufficient One, Lord God Almighty

EL ELYON

(el el-yone')

The Most High God

ADONAI

(ad-o-noy')

Lord, Master

YAHWEH

(yah-weh)

Lord, Jehovah

JEHOVAH NISSI

(yeh-ho-vaw' nis-see')

The Lord My Banner, The Lord My Miracle

JEHOVAH-RAAH

(yeh-ho-vaw' raw-aw')

The Lord My Shepherd

JEHOVAH RAPHA

(yeh-ho-vaw' raw-faw')

The Lord That Heals

JEHOVAH SHAMMAH

(yeh-ho-vaw' shawm'-maw)

The Lord Is There

JEHOVAH TSIDKENU

(yeh-ho-vaw' tsid-kay'-noo)

The Lord Our Righteousness

JEHOVAH MEKODDISHKEM

(yeh-ho-vaw' M-qadash)

The Lord Who Sanctifies You, The Lord Who Makes You Holy

EL OLAM

(el o-lawm')

The Everlasting God, The God Of Eternity,

The God Of The Universe, The God Of Ancient Days

ELOHIM

(el-o-heem')

God, Judge, Creator

QANNA

(kan-naw')

Jealous, Zealous

JEHOVAH JIREH

(yeh-ho-vaw' yir-eh')

The Lord Will Provide

JEHOVAH SHALOM

(yeh-ho-vaw' shaw-lome')

The Lord Is Peace

JEHOVAH SABAOTH

(yeh-ho-vew' se ba'ot)

The Lord Of Hosts, The Lord Of Power

www.ingramcontent.com/pod-product-compliance
Lightning Source LLC
Chambersburg PA
CBHW022122040426
42450CB00006B/806